NAVIGATING CULTURES

A Practical Guide to the Global Workplace

By Michael W. Beard and Jason Borges

Simple Group Global

Navigating Cultures

A Practical Guide to the Global Marketplace

by Michael W. Beard and Jason Borges

© Simple Group Global 2018

All rights reserved.

ISBN: 978-0692048689

Contents

How to Read This Book

Not long ago, my wife and I (Michael) toured Paris. We bought a travel guidebook to help us get the most out of our visit. At first, we skimmed the entire book and mapped out what we wanted to do and see in Paris. Then, we found ourselves sitting in French cafes flipping back and forth through the dog-eared sections of the places we wanted to see. We carried the guidebook with us to several tourist sites to read more about the actual places we were visiting. It was full of interesting facts, easy-to-read maps and helpful tips. We even discovered several places we would have otherwise never known about.

As the subtitle suggests, this is also a guidebook. The most useful way to approach this book is to sit down and read through it once quickly. It's short, so you should be able to get through it without a huge investment of time. Don't worry about catching everything the first time through. As you find yourself in various cross-cultural situations, you can go back to relevant sections of the book and find some useful tools and advice.

Preface

We may have all come on different ships, but we're in the same boat now.

Martin Luther King, Jr.

In today's globalized world, interacting with different cultures is a given. According to a recent United Nations report on international migration, an estimated 244 million people are living outside of their birth countries. These numbers have been increasing rapidly since the turn of the millennium.

We often think that migration happens to escape poverty, famine or war. This certainly represents a large portion of global migration. An estimated twenty million migrants are refugees fleeing destabilized conditions in their homelands. But that's just one slice of the pie. Many people are also moving from so-called "developed" countries to other regions of the world. In fact, over 25% of people migrating around the world are moving from North to North, North to South and West to East.

The majority of cities in the world today are international cities. Los Angeles is now home to people from about 140 countries. People in London now speak over 200 languages. And, 40% of Sydney's current population comes from abroad. However, it is not just the big cities in the West experiencing this trend. Many smaller cities and non-Western cities are seeing the same patterns play out. For example, in Waterloo, Iowa (a typical town in the "Corn Belt" of the United States), almost 5% of the population is not white, black or Hispanic. Singapore is a mirror image of Sydney with 40% of its population made up of non-native-born people. And, the growing economy in Vietnam has attracted tens of thousands of people from all over the globe to Ho Chi Minh City, Danang and Hanoi.

The days of homogenous towns and workplaces are gone. Chances are that someone from the other side of the planet is either living in your neighborhood, employed at your workplace or is one of your customers. If not, they will be soon. That's why learning how to interact, communicate and work with people from other cultures is a critical skill in today's marketplace. We hope that this book will help you to become a better neighbor, a better co-worker, a better boss and a better friend to people from cultures different from your own.

Michael Beard
Hanoi, Vietnam

Section 1: Cultural Awareness

In the name of God, stop a moment, cease your work, look around you.

Leo Tolstoy

It is quite entertaining to watch a baby who doesn't realize that his hands are part of his body. His arms flop around in sporadic movements until one hand lands on a toy by accident. The grasping reflex kicks in as he picks up the toy and swings it toward his face. As soon as his eyes catch the toy, he either laughs or cries. Either way, he is startled to see the toy hovering over his face.

A similar process happens when we interact with people from different cultures. Things we don't expect happen and catch us off guard. Some things strike us as funny. Some things cause us to hit the adrenalin button. And, some things cause us to scratch our heads in confusion.

In the first three chapters, we will work on developing our cultural awareness. Chapter 1 defines *culture* with the help of some useful metaphors. Chapter 2 explains the stages we go through while developing an "intercultural mindset." Then, Chapter 3 highlights some areas of self-awareness that can get you started on your journey across cultures.

Chapter 1

Understanding Culture

There are these two young fish swimming along, and they happen to meet an older fish swimming the other way, who nods at them and says, "Morning, boys, how's the water?" And the two young fish swim on for a bit, and then eventually one of them looks over at the other and goes, "What the hell is water?"

David Foster Wallace

Just as fish don't think about water, we humans rarely think about our own culture (unless you happen to be an anthropologist). Fish don't realize just how pervasive water is to their existence until they are removed from it. Then, the absence of water becomes painfully obvious. Likewise, we don't realize how pervasive our culture is until we've been taken out of it and put into another culture.

In this opening chapter, it might be useful to try to wrap our heads around what culture is. Experts have offered many technical definitions of "culture." Rather than repeating those academic definitions, we'll explore five metaphors to help us understand culture. We will compare culture to: a tree, an operating system, a pair of colored glasses, an iceberg and an onion. Each metaphor highlights different facets of culture.

Culture is Like a Tree

During my (Michael) years living in Central Asia, our family had a large old apricot tree in our yard. Though it provided wonderful shade during the hot summers, the main branches were quite large and leaned ominously over the mid-section of our house. Worried about the potential damage this tree would cause if it ever fell over, we decided to cut it down. It was a big job chopping down all those thick hardwood branches. However, the most challenging task was removing the root system. The root system was deep, wide and extensive.

Culture is like that apricot tree. A large fruit tree has an extensive root system we don't see that nourishes and supports the large branches, leaves and fruit we do see. The same is true of culture. Hidden deep below every culture is an extensive root system we don't see that feeds and supports the cultural behavior patterns we do see. In addition, the roots of an apricot tree will produce apricots, not other types of fruit. We might expect to see variations in the size and shape of the individual apricots, but we cannot expect to see apples growing from apricot trees. Likewise, each culture is like a specific type of fruit growing from a specific root system. Each type of fruit has its own distinctive flavor and color just as each culture has its own distinctive flavor and color. Though we will see individuals vary within a specific culture, we cannot expect to see German cultural patterns and values growing from a Japanese cultural root system.

Culture is Like an Operating System

Dutch social psychologist Geert Hofstede likens culture to a computer operating system. He says that culture is "the collective programming of the mind which distinguishes the members of one group or category of people from another." An operating system, such as Mac OS X or Microsoft Windows, is the basic software that runs your computer. It manages how your computer receives, processes and displays information. Basically, an operating system is an environment that allows for meaningful interaction between people, software applications and hardware.

Culture is similar to an operating system in that culture provides the basic environment in which groups of people interact with each other and the world around them. Just as an operating system provides a set of rules for how a computer will function, so too does culture provide a set of system rules for how we should function in society. An operating system also determines how the computer will communicate with other pieces of hardware like a printer or Wi-Fi router. Likewise, cultures establish patterns of communication between people. These patterns involve both language and non-verbal forms of communication.

Culture is Like Colored Glasses

Have you ever owned a pair of colored sunglasses? I (Michael) have a pair of yellow tinted motorcycle sunglasses. They brighten up everything and create a greater contrast between colors, which is good for night driving. During the day they reduce the glare of the sun and block UV light. But, they also add a shade of yellow to literally everything I see. This in turn changes my perception of the color spectrum all around me. The white roses become yellow roses. The green grass becomes a vibrant yellowish-green. The blue sky takes on an aqua tone.

Culture is like wearing a pair of yellow sunglasses. Our culture shapes the way we perceive and interact with reality. What we believe to be true, good and important is largely shaped by our culture. Two people from different cultures who experience the same event sometimes walk away with opposing perceptions and reactions. For example, I remember observing two Russian men engaged in what I had perceived to be a heated argument. Their voices were raised. They were waiving their arms frantically and neither one had a smile on his face. But my perception was wrong. When I asked a Russian-speaking friend what they were arguing about, he explained that they were actually having a light-hearted conversation about sports.

Culture is Like an Iceberg

Anthropologist Edward T. Hall has compared culture to an iceberg. You probably know that only 10% of an iceberg is visible above the surface of the ocean while about 90% is hidden below the waterline. Many sunken ships, most famously the Titanic, experience the danger of a seemingly small iceberg. Likewise, many aspects of other cultures are hidden below the surface. We only realize their power after we have clashed with them.

Like icebergs, cultures have a surface level that floats above the waterline in full view of every passerby. Hall refers to these aspects of culture as *surface culture* because they are relatively easy to see and distinguish from our own culture. There are things like food, clothing, language, holidays and artifacts.

In many cases, the surface aspects of a culture stir in us a sense of curiosity and adventure. We expect that the food is going to be different and our sense of adventure causes us to find pleasure in trying something new. Generally, areas of surface culture don't cause much stress because we anticipate those differences. When you travel to Vietnam, for example, you expect people to speak Vietnamese and eat rice noodles with chopsticks.

The hidden parts of culture are what sink ships. Hall calls these aspects *deep culture*. They are the areas of a culture that we don't see until we collide with them. For example, some cultures have a very relaxed view of time. Time is seen as plentiful and flexible. Showing up 30 minutes after an agreed upon time is quite acceptable and often even expected. Other cultures might have a more structured view of time. Time is a finite commodity. Showing up even 10 minutes late is seen as inconsiderate. These views of time are hidden below the surface. You don't notice them until you get upset when someone is *always* late!

We don't anticipate differences that are below the surface. Let's imagine two people, Philippe and Frank. Philippe is from an island culture where time is very elastic. Frank is a Western European and considers his time to be limited and extremely valuable. They agreed one day to meet for coffee. Though Philippe said he would meet Frank at 10:00 am, he ran into a college classmate on the street and ended up in a wonderful conversation with his old friend. By the time he reached the café to meet Frank it was already 10:45 am. Because time in Philippe's culture is very flexible, he didn't even offer an explanation for why he was 45 minutes late. Frank was irritated and felt that Philippe was being extremely insensitive and expressed this to Philippe. Philippe couldn't understand why Frank was so upset and felt that Frank was being quite unreasonable. This is just one of the many common scenarios that play out when people collide with the hidden parts of other cultures.

Culture is Like an Onion

Though the iceberg comparison is helpful, culture is more complex than just surface and hidden areas. It's more like an onion, made up of layers that lead down to a center point. Experts have identified various layers of culture and distinguish them differently. For the sake of simplicity, we will explore just four key layers: behavior, attitudes, values and beliefs. We will look briefly at each layer and see how they are interconnected. See Figure 1.

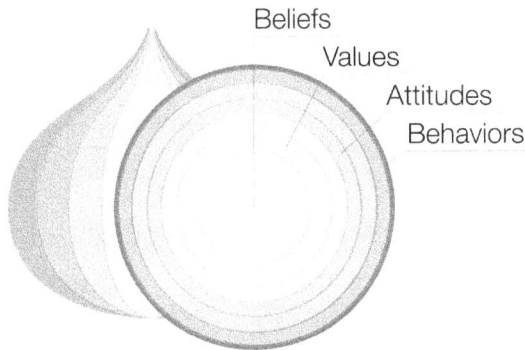

Beliefs
Values
Attitudes
Behaviors

Figure 1. Cultural Layers

Behavior: The outer layer of culture is where we find behaviors. These are surface-level activities such as shaking hands, eating spicy food and wearing turbans. Let's explore one example of a cultural behavior and see where it leads as we peel off each layer.

Most people from Eastern cultures take off their shoes when they enter a home whereas people from Western cultures wear shoes in the house. Wearing or not wearing your shoes inside a house is an outer layer behavior that differs from culture to culture. But, if you begin to ask why some cultures take off their shoes before entering a house and others don't, it will force you to peel off a layer to see what might be the cause of that particular behavior.

Attitudes: The second layer of culture is where we find attitudes. It consists of what we think and feel about everything on the surface level of culture. Easterners tend to not wear shoes inside a house because they think it is dirty to walk in from the dusty road and tromp all over the house's clean floor. An underlying attitude says that the outside is dirty and the inside is clean. In addition, shoes belong outside because they are dirty. There are also emotions connected to our attitudes. If you enter a Kyrgyz house with your shoes on, the hostess will be quite offended or consider your behavior rude. And that same Kyrgyz person would probably feel very uncomfortable if she visited the home of an Australian, who insisted that she keep her shoes on inside.

Values: What forms our attitudes? Why do most Kyrgyz feel uncomfortable wearing shoes inside whereas most Australians don't? Answering these questions requires us to peel back yet another layer to uncover the hidden values of a particular culture. A value is determined basically by what we sense is good, bad, important and unimportant. Not only that, but each culture assigns value to various things and ranks those values differently. For example, most cultures hold the value that dirty is bad and clean is good. However, cultures assign the value of cleanliness differently. Many Eastern cultures assign the value of cleanliness to the inside of a house. Likewise, everything outside the house is dirty. Many such cultures also consider certain objects like shoes and toilets to be inherently dirty. Therefore, these objects belong outside with all the other dirty things.

However, my American culture says that we can clean a toilet and clean our shoes, so it is fine to have them in your house.

Beliefs: Why do some cultures hold the value that toilets and shoes are inherently dirty? How do values of cleanliness get assigned? You guessed it. We need to peel back another layer. This is the layer of beliefs. Beliefs are the convictions that a given culture has about what is true and false, about what is real and not real. Most beliefs are handed down to us, but we rarely question them. Though you might believe that outside is dirty and inside is clean, you probably never pondered your reasons behind those beliefs. Most likely you were simply taught this from childhood and assume that it's just the way things are.

Every culture has a set of core beliefs about the world around them. These are the basic assumptions that we take for granted without questioning. For example, most of us assume that the external world outside of our mind is real and that other things and people exist. Only Cartesian philosophers and sci-fi movies like *The Matrix* question the existence of the outside world. The rest of us wake up and go about our day never doubting the existence of our neighbors, our jobs or our families.

You might be surprised to know that core beliefs differ from one culture to the next. Someone from an animistic culture might assume that the world is filled with spirits and forces of good and evil. Even most physical objects are believed to have spirits and can possess spiritual power. But in a Western, scientific, rationalistic culture, trees and rocks are merely physical objects and nothing else.

An Intercultural Mindset

Now that we have a basic understanding of culture with the help of the five metaphors presented in this chapter, we will shift our attention toward building an *intercultural mindset* in the next chapter. The first step in developing an intercultural mindset is simply becoming aware that culture exists and influences everything we do. The metaphors have helped us to develop that basic awareness. It's also helpful to think of developing an intercultural mindset as a journey rather than a destination. We never quite arrive when we set out to understand another culture. However, we grow and learn the more we explore. Our hope is that through this book you will move forward in your ability to effectively work with people from other cultures. We also hope that you will take time to enjoy the journey along the way.

Chapter 2

Shifting Mindsets

Alice: "Would you tell me, please, which way I ought to go from here?"
Cheshire Cat: "That depends a good deal on where you want to get to."
Alice: "I don't much care where —"
Cheshire Cat: "Then it doesn't matter which way you go."

Lewis Carroll, *Alice in Wonderland*

Moving Toward an Intercultural Mindset

Since the title of this book is *Navigating Cultures,* it might be helpful to know where we are headed as we navigate. Our hope is to move people from a monocultural mindset to an intercultural mindset. Cultural communications expert Milton J. Bennett created the Developmental Model of Intercultural Sensitivity (DMIS). This framework describes the various stages that people tend to experience as they build their intercultural skills. We have found this to be a useful map that explains where we are headed in this book.

The initial stages of Bennett's model are the *ethnocentric stages.* People in these stages place their own culture at the center of reality and interpret other cultures through the lens of their own. As a result, they tend to view everything from just one cultural perspective, their own. This is the essence of a monocultural mindset.

Monocultural   Intercultural
Mindset   Mindset

Ethnocentric   Ethnorelative

Figure 2. Intercultural Sensitivity Continuum

The other half of the continuum (shown in Figure 2) consists of *ethnorelative stages* of intercultural sensitivity. As people progress through them, they learn to perceive and experience other cultures beyond their own. This creates in them an intercultural mindset that enables them to function well in multi-cultural environments.

What follows in Figure 3 is our adaptation of Bennett's original model, which is available at www.idrinstitute.org.

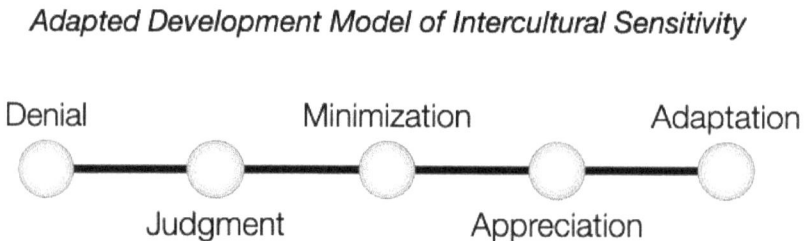

Adapted Development Model of Intercultural Sensitivity

Denial   Minimization   Adaptation

Judgment   Appreciation

Figure 3. Stages of Cultural Sensitivity

Stage 1: Denial

People in this stage are generally unaware that cultural differences exist. If they have an awareness of other cultures, it is perceived in broad categories such as *foreigner* or *minority group*. Their cultural experience is extremely limited and monocultural. All experiences are filtered through the lens of the culture in which they were raised. In today's globalized world, very few people live in this stage. Ease and relative affordability of international travel has allowed for greater contact between cultures. Additionally, the advent of the Internet and social media has further increased the likelihood of intercultural interactions, even in isolated locations.

Stage 2: Judgment

As cross-cultural encounters increase, we build stereotypes of other cultures. Those stereotypes are then judged against our own culture. Since our own culture feels natural to us, we often assume that we do things the right way and other cultures do things the wrong way. This assumption creates a critical and judgmental attitude toward other cultures. We tend to think in broad categories of *them* and *us*. Usually, *us* is superior and *them* is inferior. For example, Western cultures view themselves as civilized, developed and part of the first-world and view non-Western cultures as uncivilized, undeveloped and belonging to the third world.

Stage 3: Minimization

Though this stage moves toward a more positive view of other cultures, it tends to oversimplify cultural differences by minimizing them. It confuses reality with our culturally conditioned perception of reality leading us to believe that others experience reality the same way we do. We believe that our core cultural values and beliefs are the same in every culture. Any cultural differences are considered to be just surface-level differences. So, we tolerate superficial cultural differences such as food, clothing or greeting customs, but remain unaware of the many deep cultural differences.

Stage 4: Appreciation

At this stage, we begin to move beyond an ethnocentric perception of other cultures. Self-awareness of our own culture increases. Recognition of deeper cultural differences emerges. There is a shift away from judgmental thinking that our way is the right way. However, our non-judgmental attitude toward other cultures does not mean that we always agree with other cultural perspectives. Rather, we learn to see things from multiple cultural perspectives. We gain the ability to appreciate other cultural perspectives and patterns that we might not internalize. This stage is marked by an openness to learn and grow.

Stage 5: Adaptation

At this final stage, many cultural differences are viewed as neutral. We adopt different cultural patterns in order to fit into each new cultural environment. We build an intuitive sense that values differ between cultures. This sense leads to a more empathic attitude toward differing cultural perspectives. We can even adopt and internalize new cultural perspectives. As a result, it doesn't require much effort to move between cultures. We easily adjust our attitudes, perceptions and behavior accordingly.

Waking Up

Have you ever been jolted out of a deep sleep? You have that feeling of complete disorientation. You wonder, "Where am I?" "How did I get here?" "What day is it?" Perhaps even, "Who am I?" As your conscious mind catches up with your body, you develop greater and greater awareness of yourself. The first step toward an *intercultural mindset* is building intercultural awareness skills. These skills help us wake up to a clearer perception of ourselves and other cultures. The next chapter explores areas of awareness that impact our ability to interact with people from other cultures.

Exercise

Take a few minutes to think about the mindset model presented in this chapter. Is your mindset typically ethnocentric or ethnorelative regarding other cultures? Which stage best describes your current mindset?

Chapter 3

Building Awareness

Everything that irritates us about others can lead us to an understanding about ourselves.

Carl Jung

Awareness is the most important tool you need to develop effective intercultural skills. In this chapter, we will explore several areas of cultural awareness. We will also complete some self-evaluations and exercises to assess your awareness levels. If you are skimming through the book for the first time, have a glance at these exercises and self-evaluations. However, to benefit the most from the book, please take the time to work through each exercise.

Awareness of Strengths and Weaknesses

Several personal qualities are helpful in developing intercultural proficiency. Things like openness to other ideas, flexibility and good listening skills are valuable to understand someone from another culture. We will briefly look at 15 such qualities. As you read through each short description, give yourself a rating from 1 (very weak) to 5 (very strong). By rating yourself you will be able to identify qualities that are your strengths and weaknesses.

Most people have a few really strong areas, some glaring weaknesses and several qualities where they fall somewhere in the middle.

This self-evaluation will only be useful if you are honest with yourself. So, don't try to rate yourself as you would like to be, but rate yourself as you really are. You could also ask someone who knows you well (i.e., spouse, parent, or close friend) to rate you. If you score low in several areas, don't worry. The point of the self-evaluation is to build awareness of our strengths and weaknesses. Once you identify them, you can rely on your strengths while developing your weak areas.

Rate yourself 1 (very weak) to 5 (very strong) below each description:

Respect: How good are you at valuing others with differing or even opposing ideas or beliefs? Not just in minor disagreements (like what pizza toppings to order), but in controversial issues that you are passionate about, such as politics, morality and religion.

My Respect Rating: _____

Openness: How open are you to trying new things? How willing are you to try new ways of doing things? Are you comfortable learning from people who are very different from yourself?

My Openness Rating: _____

Tolerance for Ambiguity: Are you the kind of person who needs to have everything mapped out? Are you uncomfortable with not always knowing what's next or even what's happening now? Can you start a task without knowing all the instructions beforehand?

My Tolerance for Ambiguity Rating: _____

Flexibility: Do last minute changes to your plans stress you out or make you angry? How good are you at going with the flow? Do you see life as shades of gray, or mostly black or white?

My Flexibility Rating: _____

Adaptability: This is an extension of flexibility. Are you able to modify your communication styles or behaviors depending on who is around you? How good are you at changing your expectations to reflect new circumstances?

My Adaptability Rating: _____

Curiosity: Are you adventurous? Are you the kind of person who is drawn to trying bizarre foods? When you travel, do you like to stick with the standard tourist attractions or venture out to find where the locals go? Do you ask others about their culture?

My Curiosity Rating: _____

Suspension of Judgment: Are you able to resist rushing to judgment while you gather more information? Or, are you often quick to judge situations and people?

My Suspension of Judgment Rating: _____

Cultural Self-Awareness: How well do you know your own culture? Are there things you used to think were *natural* that now you know are just part of your culture? Hint: If you can't think of any examples, then you probably have a low amount of cultural self-awareness.

My Cultural Self-Awareness Rating: _____

Knowledge of Worldviews: How well do you understand people with different worldviews? For example, do you know some of the basic beliefs of Muslims, Jews, Buddhists and Christians? Hint: If you're not even sure what a worldview is then you're probably low in this area too.

My Knowledge of Worldviews Rating: _____

Culture-Specific Knowledge: How well do you know other people's cultures? Think specifically about your neighbor or co-worker who is from another culture. How much do you know about their culture? Do you know how, when and what they usually eat for dinner? Do you know what major holidays they celebrate? Do you know how they greet one another?

My Culture-Specific Knowledge Rating: _____

Foreign Language: Do you speak any foreign languages? If so, how well do you speak and understand those languages? Language is a huge part of culture. You learn a lot about culture through language.

My Language Rating: _____

Listening Skills: Do you seek first to understand and then to be understood? Do you listen for meaning or do you typically think about what you're going to say when the other person is finished speaking?

My Listening Skills Rating: _____

Observational Skills: Are you the kind of person who picks up on subtle facial expressions, tone of voice or body language? People with good observational skills notice non-verbal cues. They are aware of what's going on around them.

My Observational Skills Rating: _____

Empathy: Are you able to understand how people feel? Do you often share in the emotions of others? Do you have a high degree of emotional intelligence?

My Empathy Rating: _____

Communication Skills: How good are your interpersonal communication skills? Do you tend to communicate clearly, or do you often find yourself stuck in misunderstandings?

My Communication Skills Rating: _____

Let me remind you not to feel bad if you have rated yourself low on several (or even most) of these qualities. Low numbers don't mean that you are incapable of being effective in another culture. It just means that you need to grow in certain areas if you want to be effective cross-culturally. The good news is that with time and practice you can develop and grow in *all* of these qualities.

Awareness of Personal Interpretations

See Figure 4 below and write down what you think is happening in the scene. Then STOP! Don't continue reading until you have completed this part of the exercise.

Figure 4. Scene

Exercise:
Write down what you think is happening in this scene.

Do not continue reading until you have completed this exercise.

What do you think is going on in this scene? There are usually as many interpretations of this picture as there are people observing it. Why? Because the image is purposefully vague. Sometimes cross-cultural scenarios present us with vague situations where the *correct* interpretation is not clear, but our brain doesn't like fuzzy situations. So, it fills in the blanks based on previous knowledge and experience. Think about how you arrived at your interpretation. Did the image cause you to recall something you've seen before? Did it remind you of some past experience? Our brain is constantly interpreting the world around us.

Awareness of Ability to Misinterpret

Imagine one day that you are walking down the street, and you see a good friend ahead of you. You quicken your pace to catch up and tap your friend on the shoulder, only to discover when she turns around that she is not your friend but a complete stranger. We've all experienced a situation similar to this. This scenario shows that we are capable of misinterpreting things. In fact, a skilled magician makes a living off of our susceptibility to misinterpretation. He tricks us into seeing things vanish into thin air or suddenly appear out of nowhere.

Optical illusions press the point even further. They force our eyes to misinterpret what we *are* seeing even though we know what we *should* be seeing. Type "optical illusions" into an image search on Google, and you will see hundreds of very creative examples. There are two-dimensional drawings that appear to be three-dimensional. There are still images that appear to be moving. There are images that cause our eyes to see the same color as two different colors. In Figure 5, your eyes see crooked or curved horizontal lines. In reality, the lines are perfectly straight and parallel.

Figure 5. Optical Illusion of Curved Lines

Just as our brains can misinterpret what we see, we also can misinterpret cross-cultural situations. One time on a trip to Manila, I (Michael) went to a local market to buy a bottle of water. Not familiar with the exchange rate for pesos, I asked the young female clerk if I had given her enough money. She looked up at me, stared into my eyes and waved her eyebrows up and down. Thinking that she was flirting with me, I immediately blushed with embarrassment, mumbled something to her about being a happily married man, and swiftly exited the shop with my bottle of water. Later, I recounted the episode to a friend, who had been living in the Philippines for many years. He laughed at my obvious misinterpretation of the attractive young lady's gesture. He told me that in the Philippines, it's very common to respond "yes" to a question by waving your eyebrows up and down. "It's just like nodding your head up and down in American culture," he told me.

Not only do we misinterpret situations by arriving at incorrect interpretations (i.e., seeing curved lines when they are actually straight), but we also misinterpret by seeing things that aren't there at all. Look at the grid of black tiles in Figure 6. Do you see dots flickering between the tiles? If so, your brain is actually causing you to see something that isn't there.

Figure 6. Optical Illusion of Dots

We often see things in a cross-cultural setting that simply are not reality. You think someone is angry because he is talking loudly and using very expressive gestures, but he is actually very happy about something. You assume someone is happy because she is smiling and laughing only to realize that she is extremely embarrassed. You think that someone is upset with you because she won't maintain eye contact, only to realize that not maintaining eye contact is a way of showing respect.

One time while on holiday in Thailand, I (Michael) rented a scooter and took my six-year-old son out for a short ride. During the ride, my son got his leg stuck between the back tire and the red-hot muffler. He ended up with a very serious burn on his leg and was taken to a local Thai hospital. He spent about a week in the hospital and underwent a few procedures to remove the dead tissue from his leg. While he was there, he needed to have the dressing changed on his burn twice a day to avoid infection. He screamed in agony during every dressing change. As his father, I was very upset watching him suffer so much pain that I couldn't relieve. However, each time the Thai nurses heard my son scream, they smiled and giggled in response. What was happening? Were the nurses being callous? Did they actually find the situation funny? This is exactly how I interpreted their behavior from my cultural perspective. I thought they were either rude or masochistic. In reality, however, they were feeling dreadfully embarrassed. In Thai culture, people often respond to stressful and embarrassing situations by smiling and laughing, and this is a natural response for them. They can't help smiling in situations like this just as a typical Westerner might not be able to keep from crying.

There are a couple things we can do to reduce or correct our misinterpretations. First, if you are confused or alarmed by something that happens in a cross-cultural situation, try to get a cultural insider to help you reinterpret the situation. A cultural insider can be either an expatriate who understands the culture well or even a person from that culture who understands your own culture well. Cultural insiders act as a bridge between cultures and are a valuable source of practical knowledge.

A second thing you can do is to learn to suspend judgment. We interpret situations by default, so we need to train ourselves to hit the pause button and just observe. You can do this by using descriptive language rather than interpretative language. Notice how I explained the situation with the Philippine sales clerk by saying, "thinking that she was flirting with me . . ." That is a clear example of interpretative language. As soon as you start attributing meaning to behavior, you are interpreting. We need to train ourselves to separate meaning from behavior. It is helpful to strip as much of the interpretative language from your observations as possible. Then, you can start asking questions about the specific behaviors that are confusing to you. Here are a few examples of interpretative and descriptive sentences.

Interpretation

As you read each statement below, underline any words or phrases that interpret rather than merely describe the situation.

1. The man yelled in anger at the sales clerk.
2. During the conversation the woman avoided eye contact and refused to talk because she was not interested in the conversation.
3. When I tried to speak their language, they laughed at me because they think I'm stupid.

Now let's remove the interpretative language so that we end up with mere descriptions.

Description

1. The man said something to the sales clerk in a loud voice.

2. During the conversation, I noticed that the woman never made eye contact with anyone and didn't say much.

3. When I tried to say something in their language, they laughed.

Exercise: Describe a confusing cross-cultural situation you have encountered. The description doesn't need to be long; a few sentences will do. After you have written the description, read it over again looking for interpretative words that you might have slipped in unconsciously. Share your description with a cultural insider and ask her to help you interpret the situation.

Awareness of Cultural Blind Spots

Another area we need to develop is awareness of our cultural blind spots. An important skill that new drivers learn is checking their blind spots. A blind spot is an area around your car that you can't see in your mirrors, so driving instructors teach every student to look over their shoulder briefly before changing lanes to make sure that nobody is in their blind spot.

Exercise: Look at the circle and the "x" below. Now, close your right eye and focus on the "x" with your left eye. Slowly move the position of the page away from you. What happens to the circle? At some point it disappears. That is your visual blind spot.

●   ✗

Figure 7. Visual Blind Spot Test

The interesting thing about blind spots is that everyone around you often sees them clearly. When you are driving down a highway, all of the vehicles behind you can see what's in your blind spot. The same is true with cultural blind spots. Usually, everyone around us can clearly see what is going on while we remain completely oblivious.

Cultural Blind Spots Checklist

Think about the culture you want to understand better. For each of the questions below, answer either *yes, no* or *not sure* about that culture. Each question to which you answer *no* or *nor sure* is a potential cultural blind spot. After you identify your potential blind spots, ask a cultural insider about them. This is a proactive way of preventing some embarrassing cross-cultural faux pas.

1. Do you know the amount of personal space that is considered appropriate?

2. Do you know if it is appropriate to touch other people?

3. Do you know if there are people you should never touch?

4. Do people eat certain foods for luck or power? Do you know which foods?

5. Do you know of any rude or offensive gestures?

6. Do you know what clothing is inappropriate to wear inside a place of worship?

7. Do you know what direct eye contact communicates?

8. Do you know what friends do and say when they greet each other?

9. Are you aware of various existing social classes?

10. Do you understand the basic roles and expectations between genders?

11. Do you understand the expectations between older and younger people?

12. Do you know what people do for leisure?

13. Do you know if it is okay to raise your voice during a conflict?

14. Do you know if it is okay to show strong emotions publically (such as anger)?

15. Do you know how people respond when they are embarrassed?

16. Do you know if it's okay to talk to co-workers directly about their mistakes?

17. Do you know how people typically resolve conflicts?

18. Do you know how to conduct a formal meeting?

19. Do you know how to greet people in a professional setting?

20. Do you know how to be a good guest in someone's home?

21. Do you know how to be a good host?

22. Do you know if it's okay to eat alone when other people are around?

23. Do you know if it's okay to ask people about their age or personal income?

24. Do you know when it is appropriate to give gifts and when it is not?

25. Do you know what public displays of affection are appropriate?

26. Do you know if it's okay to disagree with an authority figure publicly?

27. Do you know three important holidays in the culture?

Awareness of Multiple Perspectives

In the early twentieth century, Pablo Picasso launched a movement in modern art called Cubism. Picasso deconstructed images and then put them back together on the canvas in unexpected ways. For example, he often painted his subjects from multiple perspectives at the same time. As a result, eyes, ears and noses ended up in odd places on the canvas.

The cubist technique is very helpful when we cross cultures. We need to learn to deconstruct our experiences and look at them from another cultural perspective. Learning to see things from a different perspective doesn't necessarily invalidate your cultural perspective. It is possible for multiple perspectives to be valid. Which is the valid perspective of your face? Is it your front-view, your left profile or your right profile? It is obvious that all three perspectives are valid.

What do you see in Figure 8? Some people see a black candlestick while others see a white silhouette two children facing each other. Some people see both at the same time. Which perspective is valid? The reality is that both perspectives are valid descriptions of Figure 8. There is a candlestick and there are the profiles of two children facing each other.

Figure 8. Optical Illusion of Perspectives

Police detectives at an accident scene understand the importance of multiple perspectives. They interview each witness to obtain as many perspectives as possible. The more perspectives they have, the better they will be able to reconstruct what happened. Seeing things from multiple perspectives doesn't change reality. Instead, it helps us to see reality more clearly.

Final Thoughts

Another step in building our awareness involves learning about various cultural values. Different cultures place an emphasis on different cultural values. For example, some cultures place a higher value on maintaining harmony in relationships over *brutal honesty.* On the other hand, other cultures value honesty over harmony. They prefer *telling the truth* in all situations, even if it damages relationships. In the next section we explore several pairs of cultural values that present potential areas of conflict between cultures.

Section 2: Cultural Values

It would be interesting to find out what goes on in that moment when someone looks at you and draws all sorts of conclusions.

Malcolm Gladwell

Imagine that you are sitting in a classroom with ten other students. The teacher hands each student a common potato. You aren't sure why she gave you a potato, but you assume that it will be for an upcoming activity. So, you set the potato in front of you until the teacher tells you what to do with it. An hour goes by, but the teacher never asks you to do anything with the potato. At the end of the lesson, she walks around with a bag and asks each student to return his or her potato. After collecting all the potatoes, she dumps them out on a table in the front of the classroom and then asks each student to come up and identify his or her potato. Would you be able to identify your potato? Most people find this task difficult to perform. Why? Well, most people didn't take the time to notice anything special about their potato. They just saw a potato, put it in the category of potatoes and then forgot about it.

As we move into the next section of this book, we will highlight and deconstruct various aspects of culture. We will look at each aspect in order to see some broad characteristics that differ from culture to culture. Though this is a useful activity, we run the risk of stereotyping large groups of people with these broad categories. We run the risk of seeing people like potatoes. We shouldn't assume we understand all Vietnamese people just because we understand some general aspects of Vietnamese culture. People within a given culture range across a spectrum of what might be typical aspects of that culture. For example, German culture tends to place a high value on time and punctuality. If you show up five minutes after an agreed upon time, you are late. However, I have some good friends from Germany, who joke about being "late" to everything. Their surname is Schmidt and they refer to being late as the Schmidt-factor. We also need to realize that some people are on the fringes of their culture while others are toward the middle. Every generalization has exceptions, especially in a globalized world where people are influenced by multiple cultures.

In this section, we will begin with a model of culture that includes three broad value systems: honor-shame, innocence-guilt, and power-fear. Then, we will explore cultural differences in several areas of everyday life to see how those value systems play out. More importantly, we see how these cultural values can lead to intercultural conflicts.

We should also be reminded that a particular culture is not merely the sum total of these cultural values. Many other factors influence culture such as language, climate, geography, political change and globalization. In addition, each area cannot be separated from all the others. All these areas play off each other and create a unique vibe. Two cultures can appear to be similar, yet remain very different from each other.

Chapter 4

The 3 Cultural Operating Systems

Culture is the collective programming of the mind.

Geert Hofstede

Three Cultural Operating Systems

John wants to open a successful business. He writes a detailed business plan, secures a loan from a bank and meticulously files all the legal paperwork to get started.

Liwei wants to open a successful business. He visits a special pagoda that is said to bring about prosperity and makes an offering. Then, he prays to his ancestors and buys a spirit box to set up in the reception area of his new company.

Abdul wants to open a successful business. He contacts all his friends and relatives who owe him a favor. They gladly supply him with finances and connections to the right people.

These three examples highlight the three types of cultural operating systems. Chances are your computer runs on either a Windows or Mac operating system (unless you are a techno-geek using Linux). In Chapter 1, we compared a computer operating system to culture. Just like your computer, every culture has a basic operating system—a set way of processing information. Geert Hofstede says that culture is the "collective programming of the mind." And, just like computers, cultures tend to run primarily on one of three main operating systems: honor-shame, innocence-guilt, and power-fear. These three cultural operating systems orchestrate all aspects of culture. They determine how we approach areas such as relationships, time, speech, money, food and ethics.

In this chapter we will explore each of these three cultural operating systems. Then over the next few chapters, we will unpack several of the *cultural apps* running on these operating systems. Various experts have offered several lists of cultural dimensions. Some are quite long and full of technical description. In this book, we will offer a short list of some key dimensions to consider as you work with people from other cultures.

Innocence-Guilt Operating System

The *Innocence-Guilt* operating system runs on an internalized set of principles that individuals feel compelled to follow. People tend to behave primarily according to those internalized principles rather than to external social dynamics. They feel good about themselves when they follow their principles and experience internal guilt when they break with their principles (even if nobody is watching).

Imagine this common scenario. You are shopping in a toy store with your toddler. After leaving the store and walking back to your car, you discover that your toddler has a toy in his hand that you didn't purchase. In an innocence-guilt culture, you would most likely go back to the shop to either return the toy or to pay for it. Though you might feel embarrassed to go back into the store, you would ultimately feel relieved that you were able to correct the "violation." You might even feel that it was a good opportunity to teach your toddler a lesson about honesty and integrity.

Let's try another example regarding time. Imagine that you made a plan to meet friend for coffee at 3:00 pm. Thirty minutes before you need to leave, your mother drops by to chat. You suddenly feel stressed because you know that chatting with your mother will make you late to meet up with your friend. You invite her in, but explain that you only have about 10 minutes to chat because you have to meet your friend at the coffee shop. Your mother decides to come back some other time when you are free. You feel relief that you won't be late to your appointment and you know that your mother completely understands your situation. In this scenario, the agreed upon time to meet your friend is seen as an inflexible law. Showing up 30 minutes late or canceling the coffee date would cause stress.

Honor-Shame Operating System

The honor-shame operating system places a high value on social interactions. The community is built upon a web of interconnecting relationships and social obligations. Each set of relationships has clearly defined status roles and expectations. *Good* and *bad* behavior is not determined by an internalized set of principles, but rather by social expectations and relationships. Honor is achieved when social expectations are met and shame (not guilt) results when they are violated. Thus, people act in ways that help them gain honor and avoid shame. This is often referred to as *saving face*.

Let's go back to the example of the toddler who innocently took the toy without paying for it. In an honor-shame culture, being caught in the act of stealing would bring a lot of shame and cause a loss of face. As a parent, you might feel embarrassment about going back into the store and revealing that your child did something wrong. You suspect that the shop owner will look down on you as a bad parent. So, you decide to leave the toy in the shopping basket in the parking lot in order to avoid such a loss of face.

Likewise, the honor-shame system impacts your approach to time. If your mother showed up at your door unannounced, you would feel an overwhelming sense of social obligation to invite her in, prepare a pot of tea and lay out a plate of pastries. Your friend, who has a lower social status than you mother, will of course understand your situation when you show up an hour late, or even call to cancel at the last minute.

Power-Fear Operating System

Most computer users on the planet are running either Windows or Mac OS. However, small minorities of users run the Linux operating system. Likewise, the power-fear cultural operating system is the least common of the three in our world today according to our research.

Power-fear cultures are animistic. These cultures see a world full of spirits and supernatural powers. In order to avoid evil or to obtain good fortune, they seek power through rituals, special objects and a shaman (a person with access to supernatural power).

Contemplating the toddler-toyshop scenario, someone from a predominately power-fear culture might consider the action of his child to be a bad omen. He might even believe that the toy possesses an evil power that influenced the child to take it. As a result, he might bring the toy and the toddler to a shaman who could prescribe a ritual to ward off any residual evil.

In the coffee date situation, let's throw in another element. Imagine that the night before you had a vivid dream about your mother warning you of some sort of danger. Then, she shows up unannounced the next day just as you are preparing to visit your friend. This causes you to think that perhaps going to visit your friend is the danger that you were warned about in your dream. Based on this new supernatural revelation, you might call your friend and cancel at the last minute.

Running Multiple Operating Systems

No culture operates purely under innocence-guilt, honor-shame or power-fear. This is where our computer metaphor breaks down. Though there tends to be a primary operating system that dominates a particular culture, traces of the other two systems can be found in most cultures. For example, many Western cultures tend to run primarily on the innocence-guilt operating system. However, some social environments like the military and adolescent peer pressure employ the honor-shame system. It's also not uncommon for Westerners to follow a horoscope, to seek advice from a psychic or to have a good luck charm (all examples of the power-fear operating system).

We explored a few examples in this chapter about how the operating systems impact various aspects of our culture such as time and ethics. In the following chapters we will take a closer look at these and several other aspects of culture. Since most cultures employ either innocence-guilt or honor-shame as their primary operating system, we will limit the scope of the following chapters to these two operating systems.

Chapter 5

Relationships: Equality vs. Hierarchy

*To put the world in order, we must first put the nation in order;
to put the nation in order, we must first put the family in order;
to put the family in order, we must first cultivate our personal
life; we must first set our hearts right.*

Confucius

Equality

"We hold these truths to be self-evident, that all men are created equal," begins the Declaration of Independence of the United States of America. Equality is such a high value in American culture that you will find it referenced in almost all of its founding documents. The U.S. Constitution declares that "*We the people* of the United States," are the basis of government, not a hierarchical aristocracy. And the first amendment to the constitution protects the freedom of expression for everyone regardless of social rank or status. The underlying value is that everyone's voice is equal and therefore has a right to be heard. Western culture is *egalitarian*—everybody is equal regardless of status, rank or age. Thus, individual rights and freedoms are very important.

The value of equality plays out in many arenas in Western cultures. Most Western languages have pronouns to distinguish the number of persons (for example: "she" vs. "they"). However, we do not have any pronouns to use when we want to refer to someone from a higher social status or someone older than ourselves. In English, we refer to the President as "he" and a low-income child as "he." In fact, most Americas believe that a low-income child can one day become the President if he works hard enough.

On the other hand, many non-Western languages have specific pronouns to use when referring to elders or people who hold a higher social status. One mistake Westerners make when learning non-Western languages is to use only the generic pronouns. (All those other pronouns seem *so* confusing!) However, using a generic pronoun with an elderly person or someone with a high status in the culture can come across as disrespectful and condescending.

Hierarchy

Confucius has had a tremendous impact on many cultures in Asia. At the heart of his philosophy is a set of five basic relationships: ruler and subject, father and son, husband and wife, elders and youth, and friends. Of the five sets of relationship, only friends are equal. The other four are hierarchical.

Subjects are expected to give their complete loyalty to the ruler. In return the ruler is expected to provide for his subjects. The wellbeing of his subjects further increases his already high status. Sons are expected to be obedient to their fathers. Fathers have the duty of setting the moral example and maintaining harmony within the family. Wives are expected to respect their husbands and not bring shame upon the family. In return, the husband preserves his wife's honor and provides for her general wellbeing. Youth are expected to treat elders with the same respect and obedience they would show to their own fathers. Elders are responsible for being examples in the community to follow and for teaching youth how to live an honorable life. Though friends are equal, the relationship is nonetheless based upon mutual respect. Friends are expected to protect each other's honor and to avoid actions that would cause each other to lose face.

Many non-Western cultures have systems of hierarchy similar to the Confucian model. The actual roles and relationships might differ from culture to culture, but the essence is the same. In all hierarchical cultures, those in low social positions are expected to give their loyalty and respect to those in high social positions. Likewise, those in high social positions must provide for, protect, teach, and guide those under their authority. People have an obligation, even a duty, to conform to the social hierarchy. Failure to show proper respect to an elder is not just a social taboo in hierarchical societies; it is considered a moral offence.

Self-Evaluation

This self-evaluation is a series of cultural statements about equality and hierarchy. Check each statement that you agree with to determine which orientation you lean toward.

Equality Orientation

[ ] There should be strong checks and balances for those in authority.

[ ] I feel comfortable talking to my boss like a friend.

[ ] I don't feel trusted when my superiors *micromanage* me.

[ ] Human rights are more important than national security.

[ ] I feel comfortable sharing my opinions with a supervisor, even if they disagree.

[ ] Those with authority or power should never talk down to subordinates.

[ ] Democracy is the best form of government.

[ ] All people deserve equal treatment.

Hierarchical Orientation

[ ] Strong leaders make for strong organizations and countries.

[ ] I would never question my boss directly.

[ ] I trust those in authority to make the right decisions.

[ ] National security is more important than individual rights.

[ ] I feel very uncomfortable disagreeing with my parents.

[ ] There is a natural order in social relationships.

[ ] I would not want my child to marry someone from a lower social class.

For each orientation, count how many statements you checked.

Equality: _____   Hierarchy: _____

Points of Conflict

Showing proper respect toward a person's social status in a hierarchical culture is extremely important. Many conflicts between egalitarian and hierarchical cultures surround the perceived lack of respect. Whose hand you shake first when you enter a room might communicate respect or disrespect depending on a person's social status. In Japan, maintaining eye contact with a superior is considered a challenge to his status and authority. Using the wrong pronoun or even a generic pronoun can communicate disrespect. For Westerners, this emphasis on social hierarchy can feel oppressive and unjust because they perceive that one's freedom of expression is being suppressed.

Likewise, people from hierarchical cultures can come across as egotistical and power-hungry when they interact with people from egalitarian cultures. For example, in egalitarian cultures more and more executives are women and younger men. A female executive might be deeply offended if her hierarchical counterpart avoids talking to her directly, only speaking with the other men in a meeting. Another example might involve symbols designed to communicate one's status in a hierarchical culture such as sitting behind a large desk in a big chair. These symbols might be interpreted as narcissistic in egalitarian cultures.

Many other cultural factors influence these social dynamics such as gender roles, kinship, ethnicity and geography, but the lens of equality and hierarchy is a major factor to consider in every culture.

Chapter 6

Time: Task-Focus vs. Event-Focus

Do not attack me with your watch. A watch is always too fast or too slow. I cannot be dictated to by a watch.

Jane Austen

Task-Focus

Task oriented cultures place a high value on efficiency, planning and punctuality. Time is perceived as a physical commodity like money. You can save time, spend time and waste time. Time is limited and therefore must be used as efficiently as possible to complete tasks. Productivity is extremely important. The future tends to be more important than the past or even the present. This is especially true in the business environment.

Professional meetings are generally very direct. Conversations are short and personal matters are rarely discussed. Decisions are often made during meetings. There is usually a set start and end time for a meeting. If the meeting extends even five minutes past that time, most people we begin to feel irritated and anxious about the things they had planned to do next.

When it comes to negotiations, the focus is on the specific issues and how to resolve them efficiently. Great effort is made to avoid getting "side-tracked" by other issues. Those involved want to create win-win solutions for all parties involved as quickly as possible. Successful negotiations happen when good deals are made.

Event-Focus

Event oriented cultures place a higher value on relationships. People and events are more important than efficiency and tasks. This is true in a professional setting as well. Though a meeting might have an official start time, it probably won't have a clear end time. Also, the actual start time of a meeting is when most senior people show up, not necessarily the official start time. The meeting ends when the discussion is complete or when the person with the highest status leaves the meeting. The clock does not determine the end of the meeting. If a meeting goes longer than expected, people do not get stressed out, and it is common to intertwine personal matters with professional matters during a meeting. Decisions are often made outside of official meetings among key decision-makers.

Negotiations are similar. They are navigated through relationships, not issues. If seemingly unrelated issues impact the relationships involved, those issues will be seen as relevant to the negotiation process (even if the issues are personal rather than professional). Successful negotiations happen when good relationships are made or maintained.

Self-Evaluation

Check each statement that you agree with to see which orientation you lean toward.

Task Focused

[ ] I feel stressed when I am running late.

[ ] I plan several weeks ahead of time.

[ ] I feel annoyed when someone cancels an appointment with me at the last minute.

[ ] It's very rude to show up more than twenty minutes late without calling.

[ ] I love checking off items on my to-do list.

[ ] I don't like distractions or interruptions when working.

[ ] I get annoyed when someone takes a long time at the ATM machine ahead of me.

Event Focused

[ ] I rarely check the time throughout the day.

[ ] I usually do several things at once.

[ ] I often agree to do unplanned things with other people.

[ ] I don't feel stressed when I'm running late.

[ ] I rarely feel distracted by people.

[ ] I don't use a calendar to plan personal things.

[ ] It doesn't bother me much when guests are late to my house.

[ ] I'm glad when unannounced guests show up at my house.

Count how many statements you checked.

Task: _____   Event: _____

Points of Conflict

If an event is put on a calendar, it becomes extremely important to someone from a task-oriented culture. Changing or canceling events on a calendar can be a source of conflict if *adequate time* is not given in advance of the alteration. Most relationships (even personal) are also scheduled in task-oriented cultures. For example, parents call ahead to schedule dinner with their adult children. When someone shows up at your home or office without making an appointment, he is seen as an interruption because the task-focused person feels that her time has been violated. Another point of conflict happens when meetings spend too much time on small talk or on issues not on the agenda. Generally, they want to start the agenda as soon as possible and get right down to business.

During my time in Central Asia, I (Michael) remember being very irritated when someone would show up *unannounced* at my door to ask a favor of me. I wasn't so much irritated because he wanted to ask a favor. Rather, I was irritated because he showed up without calling ahead and then chatted with me for 15 minutes before finally getting around to his request. I even had to invite some people in for tea and talk for up to an hour before they finally got around to the reason for the visit. I saw these *interruptions* as a violation of my limited time. However, after a while, I learned that my Central Asian friends were actually trying to show respect by not making their requests immediate and too direct.

On the flip side, people are not interruptions in event-oriented cultures. In Central Asia, it is common to invite someone in for tea when they show up unannounced at your home or office because there is always time for tea. Conflicts can happen when a task-oriented person wants to get right down to business with an event-oriented person. Be careful: If a task-focused person tries to push the agenda too early in a formal meeting, it might cause offense with event-oriented people. Taking time for tea and personal conversation is a sign of respect in many cultures. It is often considered rude to jump right into business because doing so fails to extend dignity to the other person.

Chapter 7

Speech: Honesty vs. Harmony

The most important thing in communication is hearing what isn't said.

Peter Drucker

Honesty

When it comes to speech, many Western cultures place a high value on what they call "honesty." Communication is factual and data-driven. Statements are either true or false. Therefore, honesty is determined by using precise, accurate and truthful language. Most speech patterns are "low context" because the meaning is primarily found in the language itself, not in that context in which the language is being used. Thus, speech tends to be very direct in low context cultures. The English language has several phrases that reflect this cultural value: "Get to the point." "Cut to the chase!" and "Don't beat around the bush!" Not speaking directly is considered deceitful and manipulative.

Harmony

Those from an honor-shame culture value harmony in communication. Overly direct communication comes across as rude because it causes people to lose face. You avoid saying "no" because doing so would disrupt relationships. In Vietnamese, for example, it is more polite to answer "chưa" (not yet) rather than "không" (no) to most yes-no questions.

There is a misconception that honor-shame cultures are not concerned about truth. Some have made the claim that saving face is more important than being truthful. This claim can be made only if truth is defined as facts and information. However, truth in honor-shame cultures is a broader concept. Truth is contextual and relational. So, it is quite possible to be truthful while asserting a false propositional statement. We have some limited examples in Western culture when we ask questions like "How are you?" Though the other person might be dealing with some major issues, she might simply answer, "Fine, thanks." We wouldn't accuse her of being dishonest if she didn't go into all of her issues at that moment. Why? Because, in most cases, the question "How are you?" functions as a colloquial greeting rather than a genuine question of concern.

In honor-shame cultures there happens to be more situations where technically false statements are not seen as dishonest. For example, it is common in Central Asia to make up a polite excuse instead of saying *no* to a request. If someone asks to use your home phone and it's not a good time because you are leaving for work, a typical response might be, "Sorry. My phone isn't working right now." Though the statement is false, it is not considered dishonest. Rather, it is a polite social construct that allows you to deny a request without causing shame to you or the person making the request. A typical Westerner might say, "Sorry. It's not a convenient time for me to let you use my phone. I'm on my way out." However, that statement might embarrass the person making the request for being the cause of an inconvenience. Additionally, the Westerner will be seen as unfriendly. To save face, someone concerned about preserving harmony will make up a simple excuse, which is considered a polite way of saying "No" or "Come back later."

This example highlights that fact that speech in honor-shame cultures is *indirect* and *high context*. Meaning is not embedded as much in the words, but in the context. A high value is placed on harmony and face-saving. Body language, gestures, facial expressions, tone of voice and even silence communicate key messages.

Self-Evaluation

Check each statement that you agree with.

Honesty Based Speech

[ ] If you have a problem with someone, you should let them know.

[ ] If I need something important, I will usually ask the person who can provide that something.

[ ] If you have something important to say, you should explain it clearly.

[ ] I don't have a problem saying "no" to people when I need to.

[ ] When someone says "yes," they should mean it.

[ ] I pay close attention to the words people use when they are communicating something important.

[ ] I believe that some conflict can be healthy and constructive.

[ ] It irritates me if someone takes a long time to get to the point.

Harmony Based Speech

[ ] In most cases, it is impolite to say "no" to a request.

[ ] I usually know what people mean even when they don't say much.

[ ] When someone has offended me, I will ask a friend to talk with that person.

[ ] If I strongly disagree with someone, I will usually be silent.

[ ] I try to choose words that will make the other person feel respected.

[ ] I often say "yes" just to be polite.

[ ] I rely on facial expressions and gestures when communicating with others.

Record the number of checked statements.

Honesty: _____ Harmony: _____

Points of Conflict

Read this dialogue. John (an American) is the manager of hotel in Phnom Penh, Cambodia. Bopha is the shift leader under John's authority.

JOHN   I need you to come in to work tomorrow, Bopha.

BOPHA   Oh . . . [*pause*].

JOHN   I need you to work the morning shift. So, please come in by 8:00 am.

BOPHA   Uhh . . . [*pause*] . . . 8:00 am, sir? [*Bopha looks down at the ground*] . . . [*silence*].

JOHN   Is something wrong Bopha? Can't you work tomorrow?

BOPHA   Uhh . . . [*pause*]. No, sir. Nothing is wrong, sir. I will try, sir. [*long pause*] Um . . . sir . . . My mother is excited to visit us sometime.

JOHN   That's wonderful. Where does your mother live?

BOPHA   She is from Siem Reap.

JOHN   That's a nice place. Please bring her by the hotel when she comes to visit.

BOPHA   Uhhh . . . Yes, sir.

JOHN   Ok. See you tomorrow, Bopha.

BOPHA   [*silence*]

The next day Bopha doesn't show up for her shift.

This is an example of a harmony-honesty dialogue gone awry. John is very direct in his speech while at the same time clueless to the indirect signals that Bopha is sending his way. To publically deny a direct request from a superior is disrespectful in many high-context cultures. If there is a valid reason to refuse the request, a face-saving dance will ensue. The fact is that Bopha's mother was coming to town and there was no way that Bopha was going to disrespect her mother by going to work for an extra shift. There was also no way that she would feel comfortable telling her boss directly that she could not do what he had asked. Bopha used body language (looking down), silence, and indirect speech to communicate her inability to come to work. Unfortunately, John missed all those clues. He was relying primarily on direct speech during the exchange. Bopha never directly said she couldn't work and even said, "I will try, sir." So, he assumed Bopha was in agreement, even though from Bopha's perspective she had communicated in a high-context manner that she wasn't coming to work the next day.

Chapter 8

Money: Independence vs. Patronage

We think we know what we're doing. / We don't know a thing. / It's all in the past now. / Money changes everything.

Cyndi Lauper

Independence

Innocence-guilt cultures place a high value on independence. Financial independence is one important aspect of this value. To be dependent upon others financially (especially as an adult) is considered either lazy or irresponsible. Children are expected to move out of their parents' home when they become adults. Parents do not want to be a financial burden on their children, so they invest in retirement plans and desire to live as independently as possible as they age. As a result, finances are very personal and private. It is considered rude to ask how much money someone earns, how much debt they owe and how much they spent on possessions they own. People are more comfortable borrowing money from an impersonal bank than from friends and family.

This mentality toward financial independence impacts many aspects of daily life. For example, it is very common to split a bill at a restaurant rather than have one person pay for the meal. People generally feel uncomfortable giving or receiving publicly. Donations by wealthy individuals to charities are often made anonymously. Likewise, those receiving financial assistance for basic living expenses do so as discreetly as possible.

Patronage

In honor-shame cultures, people are financially *interdependent*. They feel obligated to share with others, especially family. Stinginess is a vice. People exchange resources through patron-client networks—the wealthy provide security and stability in exchange for loyalty and praise. These *financial friendships* are normal and expected.

Patronage is a relationship between unequals (patrons and clients) based on reciprocity. The patron provides protection, money and resources to people in need. The client repays the patron with loyalty, praise, gratitude and honor. People seek to be in a patronage relationship because it is often the best way to get resources. This system of patronage is prevalent in most non-Western cultures.

Participating in the patron-client system is not optional; it is considered a moral obligation. Social offense and disgrace happens when a patron is *stingy* with his resources or when a client does not reciprocate. The goal of patronage is to achieve harmony and honor between patrons and clients. The patron achieves honor through generosity. The client achieves honor by giving the patron loyalty, thanks and allegiance.

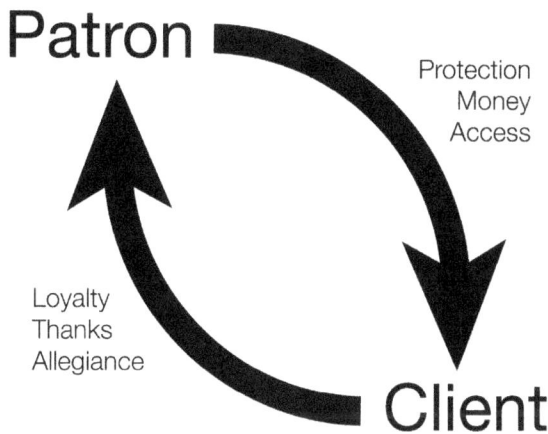

Figure 9. Patron Client Relationships

This system creates a positive feedback loop of honor as illustrated in Figure 9. Clients want to give allegiance to an honorable patron, because having an honorable patron is an honor. Likewise, the more allegiance a patron receives from clients, the more honor he possesses. Thus, honor increases on both sides as they reciprocate their social obligations.

Self-Evaluation

Independence Orientation

[ ] I prefer to use my credit card rather than to ask friends and family for small loans.

[ ] I think it is very rude to ask people how much money they earn.

[ ] Teenagers should open a personal bank account and learn about personal finances as early as possible.

[ ] You should not live with your parents if you are 30 years old.

[ ] I prefer to split the bill when going out to a restaurant with my friends.

[ ] I prefer to donate money to charities anonymously.

[ ] Rich people should not be treated differently than poor people.

[ ] I do not want to be a financial burden on my children when I am old.

Patronage Orientation

[ ] Adult children are morally responsible to house and care for their aging parents.

[ ] If I borrow money from a wealthy person in my family or community, I feel obligated to them.

[ ] When someone gives me a gift, I feel indebted to them.

[ ] It is fine to ask someone how much money they earn.

[ ] I feel obligated to give gifts to certain people in authority over me (i.e., boss, community elder, the police or people in leadership).

[ ] If I have a serious social or financial need, I will seek the help of an influential person in my community.

[ ] If I gave a large donation to my community, I would want everyone to know about it.

[ ] Gifts must be repaid.

[ ] Knowing the right person helps get things done.

Record the number of checked statements.

Independence: _____   Patronage: _____

Points of Conflict

The relational economics of patronage come into conflict with many Western values. This system can feel like dependence, corruption or manipulation. The constant requests for money or other forms of economic assistance can make Westerners feel used or annoyed.

Additionally, many in the West feel that conversations about personal finances are an invasion of privacy (and thus a violation of their independence). Asking how much money you make or how much you have in your bank account infringes on Western values because personal finances are private matters and are seen as a symbol of one's independence.

On the other hand, refusal to play the role of patron is seen as stingy in honor-shame cultures. It is common in patron-client economies for employers to pay (in addition to salaries) for employees' daily meals, to provide short vacation-like excursions, and in some cases even to provide housing. I (Michael) remember hiring a construction crew to build a business center in Central Asia. I was surprised when I had to hire a cook and allow workers to sleep at the construction site in addition to paying for the actual labor and building materials. I had become a patron by hiring a construction crew for a major project. With that role came the expectation that I would take care of my construction crew's basic living needs. Westerners in developing countries are often perceived as patrons, whether they realize it or not.

Chapter 9

Food: Efficiency vs. Hospitality

You learn a lot about someone when you share a meal together.

Anthony Bourdain

Efficiency

In most Western cultures food is a nutritional product. Eating is a nuisance or interruption to our busy days. So, eating is a task that people accomplish between other tasks. They eat while driving or they eat at their desk while working. There is no real thought process for what gets consumed. You get hungry, so you satisfy the hunger by eating something quickly. For others, food is one component of a fitness plan. These people eat to optimize their health. Whether you eat for health or in response to hunger, food is essentially a utilitarian commodity. There is nothing sacred about it.

Since food is a utilitarian activity, people often eat meals alone. Eating is functional, not relational. People eat snacks in front of others without any thought of sharing. When people do share a meal during business hours, they choose a quick place to dine for a *power lunch*. But, more often they bring food to the office so they can multi-task during lunchtime.

Food is also a form of entertainment in the West. We have media networks devoted entirely to watching the preparation and consumption of food. Most people don't watch these shows to learn how to cook the meals being promoted. They watch them purely for the entertainment value. Food becomes an exotic character to capture attention in a glamorous drama.

When Westerners prepare a meal for guests, the host tries to calculate just enough food to serve everyone, but not too much. The host doesn't want anyone to go hungry, but at the same time they don't want to be seen as extravagant and wasteful by preparing too much food.

Hospitality

In honor-shame cultures food is a form of communication. Food is highly relational and not about the nutritional value. People eat together to reinforce their group identity.

A meal is a way to bestow honor upon a guest. The more important the guest, the more elaborate the meal will be. That's why meals are a slow process. They take time to prepare and time to eat. As we mentioned earlier, even unannounced guests are invited in for tea and snacks.

After the meal, additional honor is bestowed on guests by sending them away with the leftovers. If you run out of food, you won't be able to send your guests home with a bag of food to take back to family members, and that could produce shame.

Food is also sacred in many cultures. In Central Asia, bread is a staple at every meal and is always treated with great respect. If a piece of bread accidently falls on the ground, someone will immediately pick it up and place it back on the table. I (Michael) made the mistake one time of tossing the Frisbee-shaped flatbread to a local friend while joking around. My friend became instantly upset and chided me for treating bread with such little respect.

Self-Evaluation

Efficiency

[ ] I choose what to eat for health reasons.

[ ] I sometimes eat alone.

[ ] When dining at a restaurant with a group, everyone orders his own meal.

[ ] When hosting a meal at home, it is acceptable for guests to serve themselves.

[ ] My family members eat dinner at different times.

[ ] I think it is acceptable to have a wedding ceremony without a big meal if you want to save money.

Hospitality

[ ] Eating even a small snack in front of others without sharing is very rude.

[ ] When someone drops by for a visit, I always serve them something like tea and cookies to drink and eat.

[ ] When eating at a restaurant with a group, it is common to share all the food.

[ ] I always send my guests home with food.

[ ] I avoid certain *unclean* foods.

[ ] When hosting a meal in a home, very specific places at the table are set for guests of honor.

[ ] I would be embarrassed if my dinner guest had to serve himself/herself food or drinks.

Record the number of checked statements.

Efficiency: _____   Hospitality: _____

Points of Conflict

It's difficult to give a prescription to prevent all of the potential conflicts involving food. However, there are several things to be aware of if you don't come from an honor-shame cultural background. First, realize food is deeply connected to honor. Particular foods or drinks might have special (even sacred) meaning. If you are offered a particular food or drink that is considered a source of national pride, it could be offensive to refuse it. Also, don't joke around with food or treat it with disrespect.

Second, food in honor-shame cultures is a communal activity. Eating alone or eating in front of others without sharing is often considered rude. Once in Central Asia, our organization was hosting a group of American college students for a cross-cultural exchange. One student in particular brought snacks in his backpack. During a gathering, this student innocently pulled out a granola bar and ate it in front of others without offering to share. He had only one, so it would have been impractical to share anyway. After the event, a few of the Central Asian students told me that they thought it was rude of that student to eat in front of them without at least offering to share.

Third, being a good host and guest is extremely important in honor-shame cultures. Unspoken rules exist for being a good host during a meal. These rules differ from culture to culture. Likewise there are no universal rules for being a good guest, but every honor-shame culture has rules. So, you'll need to do a bit of homework. Perhaps the best way to learn these rules is to ask someone from within the culture to help you host a meal. If you are invited to be a guest, see if you can bring a local friend along to guide you through the process.

Fourth, meetings (even informal and unplanned) often involve some sort of food. If you organize a formal meeting or invite someone into your home for a brief conversation, it is considered polite to provide at least something small to eat and drink. If food is not provided, it could communicate to the other person that you are annoyed or offended. Again, seek the help of a cultural insider to find out which foods to offer at specific types of meetings.

If you are from an honor-shame culture, be aware that food is not used as a tool of honor in Western cultures. Most meals tend to be informal. You might even be asked to serve yourself food at someone else's house or you might be presented with many choices for food and drinks. This may seem rude to you, but your hosts operate from a system that highly values independence and choice. They are trying to be polite by offering several options and by giving you the opportunity to select your own food and decide how much you want to eat.

Chapter 10

Ethics: Guilt vs. Shame

The thing to understand about shame is, it's not guilt.

Brené Brown

Guilt

Innocence-guilt cultures regulate social behavior with guilt. The government creates and enforces laws. Punishment is used as a deterrent to rule breaking. From an early age, children are socialized so their conscience causes them to feel guilty for breaking rules. These rules are abstracted from any particular context, so they can be generalized. As children grow older, this practice turns into a form of internal self-punishment when children break the rules. The result is that ethics are based on an internalized set of abstracted rules and principles. These rules and principles are then used to judge all actions and behavior. For example, providing false information is considered lying no matter what the particular circumstances might be. This situation sometimes creates moral dilemmas such as when one needs to give false information to protect an innocent life.

In a professional context, people from innocence-guilt cultures value written contracts and legal agreements. Though relationships are important, business matters rely upon a legal framework. Employee handbooks describe the rules that employees must follow. The employer carefully writes out (in precise legal language) employment benefits and expectations in labor contracts. Business deals are spelled out in memorandums of understanding and partnership agreements. Often the details of these business deals are legally binding.

Business partners and employees misbehave when they break one of the many written codes in their contracts and legal agreements. Business partners who don't fulfill their agreements are taken to court and sued. Employees' pay is docked or they are fired depending upon the severity of the infraction.

Shame

Honor-shame cultures regulate behavior with (you guessed it) honor and shame. Acceptable behavior is determined by external expectations from the community. Relationships and community determine what is right and wrong. Thus, ethics are contextual and relational. Children are taught to bring honor to their family rather than to follow an abstract set of rules. As a result there is strong motivation to seek honor and to avoid shame. Honor is secured by obtaining a positive reputation from one's social group by publicly following social expectations. Shame happens when social expectations are violated. This is referred to as "losing face." Losing face isn't just feeling bad, guilty or embarrassed about what you did. Losing face creates deep feelings of failure as a person. Social work researcher Brené Brown notes, "Shame is a focus on self. Guilt is a focus on behavior. Shame is 'I am bad.' Guilt is 'I did something bad.'"

In the context of business, relationships and reputation are very important. A business owner might choose not to do business with someone based on reputation and relationship even if he stands to benefit financially. Likewise, he might choose to do business with someone based on relationship alone even if there is no indication of a financial reward. *Whom* you do business with is much more important than *how* you do business.

Employees are usually hired based on relationship. It is very common to see large numbers of extended family members working in the same family-owned business in honor-shame cultures. Some people might be employed simply because they are family, even if there isn't a specific job for him or her.

High value is not placed on contracts and written agreements. When settling business matters, the context and people involved in a business issue can outweigh written agreements.

Self-Evaluation

Guilt Morality

[ ] Without the rule of law you cannot have a civil society.

[ ] When I do something wrong, my conscience bothers me.

[ ] I live my life by a set of internal values and principles.

[ ] It is very important to have a clear contract in business dealings.

[ ] If I know that I am doing the right thing, I don't really care what other people think about me.

[ ] Punishment is a necessary deterrent for crime.

[ ] I would never go through a red light unless it was an emergency.

[ ] I would never take a job without an employment contract.

Shame Morality

[ ] I am very concerned about what people in my community think about me.

[ ] When I do something that is embarrassing for my parents, I feel like a horrible person.

[ ] It is very important to have good relationships in business dealings.

[ ] My family's reputation is extremely important to me.

[ ] People who break social expectations suffer humiliation.

[ ] Our ancestors are highly respected in my family.

[ ] Most names in my home language have a specific meaning.

Record the number of checked statements.

Guilt: _____   Shame: _____

Points of Conflict

Probably the most common point of conflict within the context of business involves written contracts and agreements. Business people from innocence-guilt cultures are motivated to get everything in writing. They believe that if something is written down, it cannot be changed. In addition, little attention is given to the personal relationships involved in business matters. However, this is the exact opposite of how people from honor-shame cultures approach business. Relationships are most important. They trump anything on paper.

Section 3: Practical Application

Knowing is not enough; we must apply.

Willing is not enough; we must do.

Johann Wolfgang von Goethe

Now that you have a good intercultural knowledge base, it's time to practice what we've learned. These final chapters are focused on turning your new intercultural knowledge into skills. We will look at the relationship between language and cultures. Taking the time to learn even a little bit of someone's language can unlock new areas of cultural understanding. Then, we will explore how to form new cultural habits. What feels natural to you is probably just a cultural habit. When we cross cultures we need to learn new cultural habits. Finally, we will learn three simple steps to take when we find ourselves in the midst of cross-cultural confusion.

Chapter 11

The Culture of Language

If you talk to a man in a language he understands, that goes to his head. If you talk to him in his own language, that goes to his heart.

Nelson Mandela

Connection between Language and Culture

Language is not just a vehicle we use to communicate our thoughts and ideas. Language also shapes our thoughts and ideas. Anthropologists Edward Sapir and Benjamin Whorf theorized that language determines what we are able to perceive as reality. They proposed that language acts like a filter for reality. We only perceive what our language allows us to perceive. This theory was based on their research showing that languages have varying vocabulary sets and grammar for concepts such as color and time. One example involved the Native American Hopi tribe. Whorf asserted that the Hopi did not have any adequate words or grammatical structures for the concept of time. He concluded that if the Hopi did not have language to describe time then time did not exist in the minds of

Hopi people. In another example, Sapir and Whorf claimed that native Tiv speakers from Western Nigeria perceive brown, red and yellow as one color because the Tiv language only has one world for all three colors, *nyian.*

More recent research has shown that Sapir and Whorf's hypothesis went a bit too far. In the 1980s, linguist Ekkehart Milotki debunked Whorf's claim that the Hopi had no concept of time. Current studies have also shown that we are all physiologically capable of seeing the same spectrum of colors. Though you might be capable of seeing the colors brown, red and yellow, you might not see them as fundamentally different colors if your language uses only one word to refer to them. Your mind would classify them as variations of one color "nayian" instead of three distinct colors. Though language does not determine *WHAT* we perceive as reality, it does determine *HOW* we perceive, organize and classify reality. So, it filters reality to some extent.

On the positive side, learning a new language helps us to expand our perception of reality. This happens even within one's own language. Most native English speakers, for example, have a basic vocabulary for colors. However, an artist has a rich color vocabulary that describes variations in the tint, tone, and shade of colors. The average English speaker lumps a vast number of distinct colors into three broad categories: blue, light blue and dark blue. However, the artist might distinguish a variety of blues such as azure, berry, admiral, indigo, lapis, cerulean, cobalt and so on.

Let's look at another example regarding. In English, we talk about the future being in front of us while the past is behind us. Native English speakers tend to be future-oriented because the future lies in front of us. In Vietnamese, the phrase for "next week" is literally translated "the week behind you." Likewise, "last week" in Vietnamese is literally, "the week in front of you." This is the opposite of English. The past (last week) is in front of us and the future (next week) is behind us. Since the past has already occurred, we can clearly see it. However, the future hasn't happened yet and therefore it can't be seen. It is hidden behind us. Is it not a surprise then to discover that Vietnamese culture places a higher value on past-oriented categories like tradition, ancestors and the elderly? Conversely, English-speaking cultures tend to place a higher value on change, the future and youth. Does this mean that Vietnamese are incapable of planning for the future? Does it mean that they don't value the youth of their culture? Of course not. It means that traditional Vietnamese culture tends to place a higher value on past-oriented categories such as ancestors, elders and cultural traditions than English-speaking cultures and this attitude is reflected in their language.

Another example we highlighted in a previous chapter concerns the differences in pronouns between Western and Asian languages. Western languages tend to employ generic pronouns whereas Asian languages tend to employ pronouns that identify social relationships. Vietnamese, for example, has an intricate web of kinship terms that function as pronouns. You refer to people as older brother, younger sibling, aunt, and grandfather even if you were not related to them by birth. The kinship terms function not only as pronouns, but also as symbols of respect and recognition of social status. As you study the language of a target culture, you will see examples of how all aspects of culture are intertwined with its language.

Did language create culture, or did culture create language? Like the chicken-egg debate, we're not sure we can determine which came first. However, we can say that language influences culture and vice versa. Language and culture shape each other. So, if you want to gain a deeper understanding of any culture, learning the local language will open up new vistas of understanding.

Tips for Language Learning

Learning a new language can seem like a daunting endeavor. However, there are helpful strategies for learning any language more quickly and effectively.

Find Your Motivation

Being successful at learning another language is heavily dependent upon your personal motivation. When I (Michael) learned to speak Russian, I did so because I was heavily motivated. During the time I lived in Central Asia, there were very few English speakers around me. If I wanted to buy food I had to speak Russian. If I wanted to take a taxi, I had to speak Russian. If I wanted to pick up a package at the post office, I had to speak Russian. For just about everything I needed to do, I had to figure out how to do it in Russian. Therefore, my motivation to learn Russian was extremely high.

Set Language Goals and Track Progress

If you are trying to achieve something, it's always helpful to know exactly where you are headed. Start by deciding where you want to be in one year. Try to make it as clear as possible. It's also helpful to think about your goal in terms of what you want to be able to do. For example, "In one year I will be able to give a thirty-minute public speech about my company." Then, break down the larger goal into smaller related bits. For example, a first step toward that larger goal might be, "I will learn how to introduce myself in my target language." After you have a big goal broken down into smaller chunks, it is critical to regularly assess your progress. Finally, turn all of your smaller goals into a checklist of quantifiable statements that you can evaluate. A checklist for our example above might include being able to do the following:

- Introduce myself in Chinese
- Introduce my family in Chinese
- Describe what my company does in Chinese
- Describe my job in Chinese
- Describe my company's major goals in Chinese

If you recall the discussion in Chapter 6 about time, you might recognize that our advice is highly task focused. What can we say? We are products of our culture.

Fail Often

You can't learn a new language if you aren't willing to fail every day. You have to be comfortable making lots of mistakes: pronunciation mistakes, vocabulary mistakes, grammar mistakes and comprehension mistakes. Language is one of those things you learn by making literally thousands of mistakes. If you wait until you can talk fluently to speak another language, you will never learn to speak it. When we were toddlers learning to speak, we didn't start out quoting Shakespeare. Instead, we babbled out incomprehensible nonsense like "ba ba ga ga" and smiled confidently as we said it. Over time the nonsense babbling morphed into understandable words, then sentences, then stories. It's not much different learning a new language as an adult.

Listen then Speak. Read then Write

Consider how children learned their mother tongue. No babies come out of the womb talking in complete sentences. It might take from 6 to 18 months before babies start speaking their first words, but they are not inactive language learners during that time. They are absorbing a great deal of language. In fact, a child starts listing to their mother's speech in the womb. Many linguists believe that our brains are hardwired to learn any language we hear. Noted linguist Noam Chomsky has proposed the theory that the mind contains a *language acquisition device* (LAD) that predisposes the brain to learn any human language. As soon as we begin to regularly listen to a language, our brain goes to work trying to decode it. Language learners often indicate that they can understand much more than they produce in a new language. This seems to support the LAD theory.

If you want to become a better speaker, work on becoming a better listener. The same is true for reading and writing. You probably learned to recognize letters of the alphabet and basic words before you could write them as a child. It's not different for an adult learner. If you want to improve your writing skills in a second language, you need to read and read a lot.

Find a Language Helper

You don't need a professional teacher to learn a language. If you know some simple language learning activities, you can get any native speaker to help you. We will describe a few activities below to get you started.

Use It or Lose It

Did you study a foreign language in high school? If you never used it after graduation, chances are you forgot what you learned. Why? It is probably because you never had an opportunity to use the language outside of the classroom. The key point here is that you don't learn language during your language lessons. Let me say that again. *You don't learn language during your language lessons.* You learn it when you use it in real life situations. I've (Michael) studied some obscure lists of vocabulary in Russian during my formal lessons. But, the vocabulary that I know and can use effortlessly is the vocabulary that I started using in everyday life.

One way to use your language often is to find a native speaker who can meet you for coffee a few times a week to practice what you are learning. If you can't find a local native speaker, you can connect with someone online using a video communications platform like Skype. Another way is to create a daily language route. Choose a few places to visit everyday where you can practice the language with native speakers. Tell them you are learning their language and would like to practice what you are learning for a few minutes each day. Then, go prepared to practice the phrases and questions you are learning in your new language. If you need to, write your new phrases and questions on a note card. Put your language books away, and enjoy a conversation!

Employ Your Senses

Employing your five senses during the learning process increases learning ability. That's why you dissected frogs in your biology class. You can learn about the anatomy of a frog by studying a drawing, but teachers know that students are more engaged when they are standing up with a scalpel in their hands and smelling the formaldehyde of a dead frog. The multisensory experience cements the knowledge much more effectively. This is true for language learning as well. Singing songs and playing language-based games is a great way to make your language learning more active.

Another effective method is called *Total Physical Response* (TPR). You'll need the help of a native speaker for this, but your helper doesn't need to be a trained teacher. You can start with a list of verbs you want to learn like stand, sit, walk, and jump. Ask your helper to say the word in the target language. You respond by performing the action. When you hear the word "stand," you stand. When you hear the word "sit," you sit. Once you have some basic verbs down you can add other parts of speech like nouns and prepositions. For example, your language helper says, "Walk *through* the *door*." You respond by physically walking through the door.

Get Some Power Tools

Having some basic power tools in your garage can speed up the time it takes to tackle your home improvement projects. Likewise, language learning has a set of power tools as well. These are some short questions and phrases you can learn to say in your target language that can give you access to new learning on the spot without a teacher. They will help you to learn new vocabulary and better comprehend what native speakers are trying to communicate to you. Here is a simple list of useful power tools to learn in your first few weeks of language study:

- Hello. My name is [your name]. I am learning [name of target language].
- Can I practice speaking [target language] with you?

- Can you please speak slowly?
- Can you please repeat that?
- Can you write that down?
- How do you spell _____?
- What is this? What is that?
- Who is this? Who is that?
- How do you say [English word] in [name of target language]?
- How do you pronounce this word?

Always Carry a Small Notebook

Go out today and buy a pocket-sized notebook and pen (or download a note-taking app like Evernote or OneNote to your smartphone). Then carry the tool everywhere you go. As you come across new words and phrases, pull out your notebook and write them down. If you're not sure how to spell something, ask someone to write it down for you in your notebook. If you see a sign you don't understand, copy it down in your notebook (or snap a photo of it) and ask a native speaker about it later. If you're in a situation that makes you realize you're missing something in the language--a word, a phrase, how to ask a certain question--write it down and ask a native speaker about it. You can also download a voice-recording app on your smart phone and ask a native speaker to record whatever you wrote down so that you can hear and practice the correct pronunciation.

Run Some Language Acquisition Projects (LAPs)

If you are training for a race, you'll need to prepare by running some laps around the track every day. LAPs are a great way to exercise your new language and prepare for real conversations in your target language. You'll need a language helper for this. Again, your helper doesn't need to be a trained teacher. Any native speaker will do. Make a set of picture cards with related nouns and verbs you want to learn. Below are some LAPs to get you started. Be creative and develop your own LAPs as well.

- LAP 1: Look and listen. Have your helper say each word slowly three or more times while they point to an image that represents the word. All you need to do is look and listen.
- LAP 2: Listen and point. Spread the pictures on the table. Have your language helper say a word. All you have to do is point to the correct image.
- LAP 3: Listen and do. Your language helper says a simple sentence like, "The man walks." You respond my picking up a picture of a man and pretending to make him walk across the table. As your language skills progress, you can add other parts of speech to this LAP. For example, your helper could say, "Put the apple on the floor behind your chair." You respond by putting the image of the apple on the floor behind your chair.

- LAP 4: True or False. Your language helper picks up an image and asks, "Is this a [vocabulary word]?" You respond with a simple *yes* or *no*. If your helper holds up a picture of an apple and says, "Is this a banana?" You can say "No." As you learn more words, you give longer answers such as "No. That is not a banana. That is an apple." You can also add other parts of speech as your skills progress.

- LAP 5: Point and say. Next, your language helper points to an image, and you must say what it is. As you progress, have your language helper select several images. Then, you respond by saying a complete sentence that describes all of the words represented by the images.

Watch Movies

There are two keys to learning language by watching movies, especially early on in your language development. First, watch movies that you've seen a few times in your native language. If you try to watch a movie you haven't seen before in a foreign language, you are going to spend a lot of energy just trying to follow the storyline. If you already know what's going to happen in the movie, you can expend your mental energy to listen for new vocabulary and phrases. Second, turn on the subtitles in the target language (not your native language). Subtitles are great. They visually reinforce what you are hearing and they help to increase your reading ability. You don't want to use subtitles in your native language because it conditions your mind to constantly translate. You need to train your mind to *think* in the target language, not to translate.

Ask Smart Dumb Questions

A smart dumb question is a question that you already know the answer to like, "How do you make a cup of tea?" Since you already know the answer, you don't need to focus on understanding the answer. Instead, you can focus on how a native speaker would answer the question in the target language. You can even pull out your phone and video record their answer and review it later. Even better, ask your language helper to make a cup of tea with you while slowly explaining how to make a cup of tea. Here are some more examples of smart dumb questions:

- How do you brush your teeth?

- How do you make the bed?

- How do you operate the washing machine?

- How do you make a phone call?

- How do you wash the dishes?

- How do you make a bowl of oatmeal?

Cultural Patterns

Language is a culturally conditioned pattern of speaking and writing. We learn to use specific sounds and symbols to express our thoughts to people who speak and write the same language. Learning a new language is basically learning a new system of sound and symbol patterns. However, language is not the only system of culturally conditioned patterns. All cultures have patterns of behavior. Repeating a patterned way of doing something eventually forms a set of habits. In the next chapter, we will turn our attention to habits and explore the relationship between habits and culture.

Chapter 12

New Cultural Habits

We are what we repeatedly do.

Aristotle

Culture and Habits

Most of culture is actually a system of acquired habits. They are automatic behaviors that people do without thinking. For example, you probably don't think much about the behavioral patterns you employ when greeting someone from your own culture. It just feels natural to you to shake hands, kiss on the cheeks or bow. Because habits feel natural, we tend to confuse our cultural habits with human nature. Therefore, a simple definition of culture could be: "the way we usually do things."

If you are an experienced motorist, driving a car probably feels natural to you as well, but think back to when you first learned how to drive. You probably confused the brake and accelerator pedals a few times or turned on the windshield wipers when you meant to signal a lane change. You carefully watched the cars around you and paid close attention to the traffic signs and signals. Most likely, you even felt stressed and tired after just a bit of driving. Over time, however, you developed a set of driving habits. In fact, your driving habits became so efficient that you don't even think about driving while you are doing it. You now drive by habit without giving much thought to the actual process of driving. Your brain literally goes into "autopilot" mode when you get behind the steering wheel.

This chapter explores what habits are and explains how we can form new cultural habits. Functioning in a new culture can become "second nature," just like driving. But first, we must understand how our brain develops habits.

The Habit Loop

Many studies have recently been conducted on the formation and anatomy of habits. Researchers now tell us that habits are stored in the basal ganglia section of the brain. This is also where automatic behaviors such as eye movement are regulated. It is an efficient part of our brain that doesn't burn a lot of energy. It is unlike the prefrontal cortex, which is the *thinking* part of the brain. It burns a lot of energy. If you feel tired after practicing a new skill like playing the piano, it is because your prefrontal cortex is on overdrive. As you become more proficient at a new skill, your brain stores that in the basal ganglia and begins to form a habit. The following diagram explains how you form new habits.

Figure 10. Habit Loop

Trigger

Habits begin with a trigger. A trigger is a cue that initiates an automatic behavior. Someone extends his hand toward you, and that triggers a culturally preprogrammed response.

Action

Your response of extending your hand to meet the other person's hand in a handshake is a culturally preprogrammed action. We perform these actions without thinking.

Reward

Some type of reward usually follows actions that are the result of habits. In the handshaking example, it might be a smile or a positive emotion. Rewards are key to habit formation. People develop bad habits like smoking because of the physical and emotional rewards they receive from smoking a cigarette.

Investment

Once a reward is experienced, it reinforces the habit loop. This causes the brain's investment in further automating the process. Investment ensures that the habit loop will eventually start on autopilot.

Conflicting Habit Loops

Cross-cultural conflict often happens when your cultural habit loops are upset. You experience a trigger that sets one of your habits into operation, but the automatic response doesn't fit the culture. You end up with either no reward or a negative response. For example, let's assume you come from a culture that has a habit system for waiting in lines at banks. You walk into a bank in a culture that has a very different habit loop. You want to speak to the bank teller, and you spot what looks a line. That's your trigger. Your *single-line formation* habit loop kicks in and you automatically walk to the back of what you think is a line. Then, you wait for the reward of moving forward to get some cash from your bank account. Instead of moving forward however, you find yourself moving further and further away from the teller. People seem to ignore the line altogether and walk right up to the teller's window. Instead of a reward, you receive a negative response.

Culture Shock and Habit Loops

Now that we understand the basic structure of a habit loop, we can diagnose what causes culture shock. Culture shock is essentially a disruption in our cultural habit loops. When the rewards our brains anticipate are denied after performing a habitual action, we experience culture shock. Culture shock can be mild when we are simply denied an anticipated reward. It can feel strong when we are not only denied a reward, but when we receive a negative reaction instead. If you extend your hand to greet someone and they respond with a confused stare, your reward is denied and replaced with a negative reaction.

Forming New Habit Loops: Stop, Explore, Act (SEA)

When you enter a new cultural environment, you should be aware that you are going to encounter cultural habit loops that are very different from your own. Building new habit loops is vital to the process of functioning well in a new culture.

Cross-cultural conflicts indicate areas where we need to adjust if we want to function effectively long-term in another culture. The final part of this chapter will guide you through the process of adjusting to new cultural habits. Think of crossing cultures as crossing a *SEA* that separates your home culture from your host culture. The acronym S-E-A stands for three simple steps involved in navigating through various new cultural situations: Stop, Explore, Act.

Stop

The first step is perhaps the most difficult. It is difficult to stop yourself from reacting when your cultural habit loops are disrupted. Judgment comes naturally to us because we have been programmed by our cultural upbringing and experiences to interpret situations in a certain way. This is why it is so important (though difficult) to withhold judgment. Stop means telling our mind to "Pause just a minute, and don't fill in all the blanks quite yet." Pausing and suspending judgment allows us to become better aware of the situation. It also creates space for us to explore our own cultural assumptions.

For example, in U.S. culture, bill collectors don't show up at your home at 7:00 pm (dinner time) and expect you to pay them in cash. In fact, some cities even enforce laws to prevent these collection methods. So, when a bill collector shows up at your house in Hanoi at 7:00 pm, you might jump to a conclusion and think that someone is trying to pull a scam. The urge to judge is often high, especially when you're experiencing tense emotions. Yet, this is exactly when we need to suspend our judgment and explore some clues.

Explore

The good news is that you don't need to suspend judgment forever. That would be pointless. The purpose of suspending judgment is to create space to explore cultural clues. Here are some clues you could explore in the bill collector example above. Is the bill collector going door to door, or did he just show up at your house? Is your host culture predominately a cash-based culture? Is it possible to ask the bill collector to come back tomorrow or pay at the office when you have a chance to get cash from your bank?

Once you have stopped for a moment, you can observe the situation. Collect as much information as possible. What are the circumstances surrounding the situation? Who is involved? What are other people doing? Are there any environmental, social, religious or other factors involved? If you don't intentionally pause and ask these questions, your mind will automatically answer them based on your own cultural values.

Stopping for a moment also allows you to assess *your own* cultural values. Take a moment to discern how the situation might be triggering a habit loop. Ask your head: What was my immediate reaction? What was I expecting to happen? How did others react?

Remember, cross-cultural situations often evoke strong emotions in us. So also ask your heart: What emotion(s) am I feeling? Why am I feeling that emotion? Do others feel the same way as I do? Our emotions influence our cultural judgments more than our rationality; therefore, emotional self-awareness is a key part of cultural intelligence.

Act

Finally, you need to assess the clues you have collected and choose a course of action. Finding a trustworthy cultural insider is extremely helpful when you are trying to assess the situation. Observe what the neighbors do, and then talk with a local friend about how to pay utility bills. As it turns out, in Hanoi utility companies send collectors out monthly to collect payments in cash because very few people have bank accounts or credit cards. You might find out that all of your neighbors do in fact pay cash on the street to a bill collector. You might also learn that they come around 7:00 pm because that is when most people are home from work.

So remember to cross the cultural SEA the next time you find yourself in a confusing cultural situation. Stop, Explore, Act—the three simple steps for reducing many cultural conflicts.

Final Thoughts

Navigating cultures can be difficult. At times you feel like you are drowning in a storm. From personal experience, we both know the stress of adjusting to a new culture. But, having learned to live and work in a new culture, we can confidently say the rewards far outweigh the costs. We hope this book helps you chart your course as you explore and navigate cultures.

Selected Bibliography

Bennett, M.J. (1986) "A developmental approach to training for intercultural sensitivity," *International Journal of Intercultural Relations*, 10(2), pp. 179–196.

Bennett, M.J. (1998) *Basic concepts of intercultural communication: Selected readings*. 8th ed. United Kingdom: Intercultural Press.

Duhigg, C. (2012) *The power of habit: Why we do what we do in life and business*. New York: Random House Publishing Group.

Hall, E.T.T. (1973) *The silent language*. New York: Bantam Doubleday Dell Publishing Group.

Hall, E.T.T. (1997) *Beyond culture*. New York: Knopf Doubleday Publishing Group.

Hofstede, G.H. (2004) *Cultures and organizations: Software of the mind; [intercultural cooperation and its importance for survival]*. 2nd edn. New York: McGraw-Hill Professional.

Hofstede, G.J., Hofstede, G. and Pedersen, P.B. (2002) *Exploring culture: Exercises, stories and synthetic cultures*. Yarmouth, ME: Intercultural Press, Inc.

Kohls, R.L. and Kohls, L.R. (2001) *Survival kit for overseas living: For Americans planning to live and work abroad.* 4th edn. London: Published by Nicholas Brealey Pub. in association with Intercultural Press, Yarmouth, Maine.

Lewis, R.D. (1999) *When cultures collide: Managing successfully across cultures.* 2nd ed. London: Nicholas Brealey Publishing.

Lewis, R.D. (2003) *The cultural imperative: Global trends in the 21st century.* Boston, MA: Intercultural Press, Inc.

Livermore, D.A. and Van Dyne, L. (2009) *Leading with cultural intelligence: The new secret to success.* New York: AMACOM American Management Association.

Nisbett, R.E. (2005) *The geography of thought: How Asians and Westerners think differently ... And why.* London: Nicholas Brealey Publishing.

Samovar, L.A., Porter, R.E., McDaniel, E.R. and Roy, C. (2012) *Communication between cultures.* 8th ed. Boston, MA, United States: Wadsworth Cengage Learning.

Storti, C. (2008) *The art of crossing cultures.* 2nd ed. Boston, MA: Intercultural Press.

NAVIGATING
Business Series

The **NAVIGATING Business Series** has grown out of decades of experience in small business development and cross-cultural work spanning North America, Central Asia, Southeast Asia and Africa. From technology and design, education, advertising and publishing, coffee, tea and online retail, our leadership team has combined their knowledge and expertise to bring you practical insights and principles that can be applied to a multitude of marketplace challenges.

Visit www.navseries.com to learn more about other topics under the Navigating Business Series.

About the Authors

Michael W. Beard is a co-founder of Simple Group Co., Vietnam. He holds a Masters Degree in Intercultural Studies from Grace College and has worked cross culturally in Central Asia and Southeast Asia for almost 20 years. His professional experience includes education, small business development and entrepreneurship. Michael has four TCKs (third culture kids) who have been raised in Asia. His wife, Michelle, is a primary school teacher at an international school in Hanoi. They have been married for 27+ years. Michael considers himself a global nomad exploring business, culture, faith and community transformation.

Jason Borges works as a cultural trainer for an American non-profit organization. He holds a Masters Degree in Intercultural Studies from Biola University and has lived in Central Asia for 10 years. His professional experience includes financial services, micro-enterprise development, and community development. Jason and his wife have 3 daughters.

www.ingramcontent.com/pod-product-compliance
Lightning Source LLC
Chambersburg PA
CBHW050511210326
41521CB00011B/2413